David A. Roozen
Hartford Seminary Foundation

The Churched and the Unchurched in America

A Comparative Profile

GLENMARY RESEARCH CENTER/WASHINGTON, D.C.

GRC A-57 / P-133
April, 1978

International Standard Book Number: 0-914422-07-3
Library of Congress Catalog Card Number: 77-94682

Preface

Both in concept and production this publication has been a joint project of the Glenmary Research Center and the Hartford Seminary Foundation. My special thanks to Rev. Bernard Quinn, Director, Glenmary Research Center and to Dr. Jackson W. Carroll, Coordinator for Research, the Hartford Seminary Foundation, for their continued support and counsel. Special thanks also to W. Clark Roof, of the University of Massachusetts, and his assistant, Richard Morse, for their help in compiling the tables which form the heart of this profile.

I am also indebted to the Rev. David Dickerman, my good friend and pastor, for providing a most thoughtful critique of an initial draft of this manuscript; and to Amy Beveridge, who acted alternately as statistician, editor, and typist throughout the preparation of the profile.

Data cited in the profile has been made available by the National Opinion Research Center as a part of the National Data Program for the Social Sciences. Computer services have been provided by the University of Massachusetts, Amherst.

David A. Roozen
The Hartford Seminary Foundation

Contents

Tables

1. Introduction

In the mid-1960's, we witnessed an unprecedented event in the life of the American Church. For the first time since records allow us to recall, many of the dominant Christian denominations actually declined in total membership (among them, Episcopalian, United Methodist, United Church of Christ, United Presbyterian), and the rate of growth for most others dropped below that of the population as a whole (like Presbyterian U.S., Christian Reformed, Missouri Synod Lutheran, and Roman Catholic). Not surprisingly, national church attendance figures also showed significant declines. These declines were especially dramatic for Catholics.[1] America was becoming (and according to most indicators is continuing to become) increasingly unchurched.[2]

A multitude of theories have been offered to explain the declines. Some claim it is an unavoidable and perhaps temporary consequence of the changing age structure

---

1. For a comprehensive review of recent trends in American religion, see Jackson W. Carroll, "Continuity and Change: The Shape of Church Life in the United States, 1950-1975," in Carroll, Johnson, and Marty, Religion In America: 1950-Present (New York: Harper and Row, forthcoming).

2. Conservative estimates would put the current number of unchurched in America somewhere in the range of 50 to 80 million.

of the population as a whole, and the declining fertility rate.[3] Others point to a
sweeping reorientation of cultural and/or personal values.[4] Still others point to the
failure of the Church to make life meaningful in ultimate terms.[5] Still others point
more directly to denominational policies, such as the intentional decision on the part
of some to decrease their traditional emphasis on evangelism in favor of an increased
concern with social activism.[6] Within Catholicism, both the "liberalizing" thrust of
Vatican II and the "conserving" thrust of Humanae Vitae have been villainized with
equal vigor.[7]

The fact is, however, that despite both speculation and an increasing number of
sociological and denominational studies, we still do not know what forces are at work.[8]
Nor do we know what to expect in the future. Even more perplexing for those concerned
that the Church reach out to the unchurched is the fact that we do not yet have a clear
picture of just what the growing unchurched segment of the population looks like--who
the unchurched are.

To be sure, past research offers a number of wide-angle glimpses and tele-
photo circumscriptions of the unchurched and how they differ from the churched.
National surveys, for example, confirm that (when compared to the population as a
whole) the unchurched are more likely to be: males; young adults; unmarried persons;
manual workers; those who are not high school graduates; those living in cities of over

3. See, for example, W. Widick Schroeder, "Age Cohorts, the Family Life
Cycle, and Participation in the Voluntary Church in America: Implications for
Membership Patterns, 1950-2000," The Chicago Theological Seminary Register 65
(Fall, 1975): pp. 13-28.

4. See, for example, Jackson W. Carroll and David A. Roozen, Religious
Participation in American Society: An Analysis of Social and Religious Trends and
Their Interaction (unpublished report of the Hartford Seminary Foundation compiled
for the United Methodist Board of Discipleship).

5. See, for example, Dean M. Kelley, Why Conservative Churches Are Growing
(New York: Harper and Row, 1972).

6. See, for example, Warren J. Hartman, Membership Trends: A Study of
Decline and Growth in the United Methodist Church, 1949-1975 (Nashville: Discipleship
Resources).

7. See, for example, Andrew M. Greeley, "Council or Encyclical," Review of
Religious Research 18 (Fall, 1976), pp. 3-24.

8. A considerable number of studies of church membership and participation
have recently been completed. References for most of these are included in Appendix
B. In addition to these recently completed studies, there are at least two major pro-
jects presently in the works. One is a study of trends in church membership and
participation being conducted by the Hartford Seminary Foundation under the sponsor-
ship of Lilly Endowment, Inc. It involves a working group of 25 social scientists,
denominational researchers, historians, and theologians and will eventuate in a
national symposium and several publications. The second project, an ecumenically
sponsored national survey of "churchless Americans," is scheduled to go into the
field in February, 1978. Information regarding this latter project can be obtained from
Peggy L. Shriver, Office of Research, Evaluation and Planning, National Council of
the Churches of Christ in the USA.

50,000 people; and those living in the Pacific Coast states.[9] Nationwide surveys also confirm that the unchurched are less likely to assent to traditional Christian doctrine, less likely to engage in private devotions, and less likely to report religious experiences.[10]

More intensely focused studies, typically employing depth interviews, indicate that the vast majority of the unchurched can articulate with considerable specificity why they are not involved in the life of any Church. Unfortunately, the reasons articulated for non-affiliation are so varied and complex as to defy easy and/or useful summation. J. Russell Hale's recent Who Are The Unchurched? stands as the most ambitious and helpful study in this regard.[11] Reflecting on conversations with 165 persons in six heavily unchurched counties in the United States, Hale identifies 12 types and sub-types of the unchurched. The 12 types include: the anti-institutionalists; the burned-out; the boxed in; the cop-outs; the nomads; the pilgrims; the scandalized; the uncertain; the locked-out; the happy hedonists; the publicans; and the true unbelievers. Although intentionally providing no estimates of numbers, Hale believes that the publicans (i.e., those who feel the churches are primarily populated by hypocrites, phonies, fakers, and the like) constitute by far the largest group of the unchurched. He reports encountering few true unbelievers.

THE CHURCHED AND THE UNCHURCHED: A COMPARATIVE PROFILE

In what follows, we present an extensive, quantitative profile of the unchurched (and how they differ from the churched), using a unique set of cross-sectional national surveys. Using these surveys, we provide comparative data on over 150 social characteristics, beliefs, and attitudes for Protestant and Catholic churched and unchurched, as well as for those indicating no religious preference whatever. As with any profile, we make no claim to present a whole picture. Many things are highlighted, but many others remain hidden. And, like any picture, our profile is considerably more descriptive than analytical, although the comparative format in which the data is presented does allow for some inference. The profile is drawn primarily with numbers, although a brief summary text is provided. The profile is drawn with numbers because their use provides for maximum efficiency and minimum distortion in the presentation of the enormous amount of information at our disposal.

---

9. See, for example, Religion in America 1976 (Gallup Opinion Index, Report No. 130); and Marty, Rosenberg, and Greeley (eds.), What Do We Believe? (New York: Meredith Press, 1968), pp. 276-277.

10. See, for example, Morten B. King and Richard A. Hunt, "Measuring the Religious Variable: National Replication," Journal for the Scientific Study of Religion 14 (1975), pp. 13-22; and Rodney Stark and Charles Y. Glock, American Piety: The Nature of Religious Commitment (Los Angeles: University of California Press, 1968).

11. J. Russell Hale, Who Are the Unchurched? An Exploratory Study (Washington, D.C.: Glenmary Research Center, 1977).

How seriously can one be expected to take the findings of such a quantified profile? To paraphrase what Andrew Greeley has said in another context, the proper response is neither to reject them completely nor to accept them unreservedly. Like all survey research, the findings constituting our profile tell us something, and tell us something relatively important. They give us important hints, but they tell us considerably less than we need to know. For example, our profile indicates a clear tendency for the churched to be less supportive of civil liberties than the unchurched. This finding cannot simply be dismissed. It ought to be a matter of serious reflection and more careful research. But, neither can it be asserted as a phenomenon proved beyond all reasonable doubt.[12]

FIVE CATEGORIES OF CHURCHED AND UNCHURCHED AMERICANS

Up to this point, we have used the terms "churched" and "unchurched" loosely, as if they had some commonly agreed upon and taken-for-granted meaning. A review of the relevant literature, however, indicates that any such consensus exists only at a very general level. It is important, therefore, to define the terms.

It is commonly agreed that to be "churched" implies some kind of participation in or association with the ongoing life of a local religious institution, i.e., a con-gregation, a parish, a synagogue, a tabernacle, a mosque, etc. The emphasis is on "belonging" or "involvement" as opposed to "believing" or "faithfulness." Consensus, unfortunately, breaks down at the point of specifying just what kind of and/or how much involvement is necessary to distinguish the churched from the unchurched. Is it simply holding membership? Is it baptism? Is a certain level of participation at worship services or other church activities necessary? Or is it some kind of more subjective phenomenon, like the extent to which one's everyday life is nurtured and informed by a community of faith? We do not intend to debate here which criteria are most appropriate. Suffice it to say that for better or for worse, most past research has employed either membership or some level of church attendance as its criterion.

The distinction between churched and unchurched made in our profile involves two criteria, and provides us with five mutually exclusive categories.

1. The Protestant Churched

2. The Protestant Unchurched

3. The Catholic Churched

4. The Catholic Unchurched

5. Those Expressing No Identification with Any Religious Institution

---

12. Marty, Rosenberg, and Greeley, op.cit., pp. 116-117.

Protestant, Catholic, or no religious identification is determined for the purposes of
our profile by a respondent's answer to the following question: "What is your religious
preference, is it Protestant, Catholic, Jewish, some other religion, or no religion?"
Those indicating a "Jewish" preference or a preference for "some other religion" are
not considered in the profile because of their extreme infrequency. Those indicating
no religious preference constitute one of our five categories, a type which we consider
to be unchurched.

Churched and unchurched Protestants and Catholics are differentiated in terms of
their response to the following question: "How often do you attend religious services?"[13]
Those indicating they attend "about once a year" or less are classified as unchurched.
Those indicating they attend more than "about once a year" are classified as churched.

Estimates of the percentage of the American population who are unchurched
generally fall between 25 and 40 percent depending on the definition and data source
used. This means that somewhere between 50 and 80 million Americans are unchurched.

The numbers and percentages of our five churched and unchurched types, plus
Jewish and "other religion" respondents whom we deleted from the profile, are as
follows (based on our total sample, N = 7,590):

	Protestant Churched	Protestant Unchurched	Catholic Churched	Catholic Unchurched	No Religious Preference	Deleted from Profile
Percent	44	19	19	6	7	4
(N)	(3360)	(1465)	(1449)	(476)	(505)	(335)

Combining our three unchurched categories (the Protestant unchurched, the Catholic
unchurched, and those with no religious preference) puts our total estimate of the
unchurched in America at 32 percent of the population. This falls almost at the mid-
point of the range of previous estimates.

_____

13. The question used a nine-category forced-choice response format. The
nine categories were: never; less than once a year; about once a year; several times
a year; about once a month; two-three times a month; nearly every week; every week;
and several times a week. Those not answering or those indicating that they did not
know have not been included in the calculation of our tables except where noted.

THE DATA

The data for our profile come from the 1972-1976 General Social Surveys of the National Data Program for the Social Sciences.[14] This series of surveys is unique in many respects, but for present purposes two features in particular are worthy of note. First, each survey in the series uses a standard questionnaire with identical questions appearing every year or at least every other year. Since each survey contains approximately 1,500 interviews, combining the five surveys in the series provides a minimum sample of 3,000 for any question included in the series, and a possible sample of 7,590 for any question included in each of the five surveys.[15] The availability of such large samples enables one to consider characteristics of groups that otherwise appear in insufficient numbers in national surveys for meaningful presentation. Of the five categories of churched and unchurched included in our profile, unchurched Catholics and those with no religious identification would normally fall into this category. For our purposes, the second unique feature of the series of social surveys is the content of the questions included. Not only do they cover as wide a spectrum of general social characteristics and attitudes as can be found in any national survey (almost 200 individual items), but they also include a significant number of questions on religion.

The survey data come from personal interviews administered in March of each respective year to a national cross-sectional sample of non-institutionalized adults, 18 years of age and older. Each survey contains approximately 1500 respondents selected according to a multi-stage probability sampling design.[16] Estimates of sampling error can be found in Appendix A.

OUTLINE OF THE PROFILE

Of the almost 200 questions contained in the rotational scheme of the General

---

14. More detailed information regarding the National Data Program for the Social Sciences and its series of General Social Surveys can be found in: National Data Program For the Social Sciences (Chicago: National Opinion Research Center, 1977).

15. In pooling surveys spread over a five-year period we assume that any change that might have taken place over time is negligible or random. A check of the percentage of those who indicated attending religious services "about once a year" or less in each of our surveys shows that such an assumption is at least tenable for this critical variable. The percentages range from a low of 30 percent in 1972 to a high of 35 percent in 1976. For the remaining three years, the percentage held constant at 34 percent.

16. Detailed sampling information is contained in the respective codebooks for each General Social Survey. Codebooks are available through either the National Opinion Research Center, University of Chicago, 6030 South Ellis Avenue, Chicago; or the Roper Public Opinion Research Center, Williams College, Williamstown, Mass.

Social Surveys Series, 150 have been selected for inclusion in the profile.[17] In composing the profile, these 150 items have been arranged into five major sections. The first section, "Where the Churched and Unchurched Came From," focuses on the pre-adult situation of the churched and the unchurched. The second section, "Social Location," deals with the current situation of the churched and unchurched within the prevailing social structural features of our society. This section contains three sub-sections: (1) standard demographic items; (2) organizational memberships; and (3) items dealing with sociability.

The third major section, "Religious Characteristics," taps such areas as the religious belief, loyalty, and identity of the churched and unchurched. The fourth section, "Quality of Life," focuses on subjective evaluations of life experiences and alienation from traditional societal norms. The final section, "Attitudes," examines dispositions toward a wide range of personal and national issues including, for example, the death penalty, busing, the legalization of marijuana, pornography, feminism, civil liberties, and desirable qualities for a child. In each section and sub-section, we provide a short introductory and summary statement followed by a series of percentage tables.

SAMPLE PERCENTAGE TABLES

The heart of our profile is its series of percentage tables which show the distribution of each of our five churched and unchurched categories on over 150 social characteristics, beliefs, and attitudes. All tables follow one of two general formats. An example of Type I, the most frequently used format, is as follows:

FORMAT FOR TYPE I TABLE: SAMPLE

REGION OF RESIDENCE OF THE CHURCHED AND UNCHURCHED

	PROTESTANTS		CATHOLICS		NO RELIGIOUS PREFERENCE
	Churched	Unchurched	Churched	Unchurched	
REGION					
Northeast	13	17	38	43	24
Midwest	29	30	31	22	26
South	45	32	17	13	19
West	13	22	15	21	30
(N)	(3365)	(1468)	(1450)	(476)	(507)

---

17. For the most part only questions of a repetitive nature were not included in the profile. For example, each General Social Survey contains at least six different questions dealing with a respondent's working-occupational status. Of these six, only one is included in the profile.

Each column of numbers represents a different churched or unchurched category. These vertical columns do not change from table to table. Each row of unbracketed numbers represents a different category of the specific social characteristic being looked at. The row of bracketed numbers represents the total number (N) of respondents for each churched or unchurched category for which we have data on this social characteristic.[18] Any given unbracketed number, therefore, represents the percentage of its respective churched or unchurched category that falls into the respective category of the social characteristic under consideration. For example, the top left hand unbracketed number is the percentage of churched Protestants who live in the East. The percentage is 13. Continuing down this same column, we see that 20 percent of churched Protestants live in the Midwest, 45 percent live in the South, and 13 percent live in the West. Note that the percentages in any column add to 100 percent--plus or minus one percent due to rounding error. The bracketed number at the bottom of the column (3365) is the total number of churched Protestants on whom these column percentages are based, (that is, the total number of churched Protestants for whom we have regional data).

Type I tables are designed to provide direct answers to two general categories of questions. First: What percentage of a particular churched or unchurched type has a specific social characteristic? For example, what percentage of those who have no religious preference live in the West? The answer, as indicated in the sample table above, is 30 percent. Please note that this is not the same question as: What percentage of those who live in the West have no religious preference? The answer to this question is not directly provided in the table, although it can be calculated from the data presented in the table, and will not be the same as the answer to the first question.[19] Performing the necessary calculations indicates that 12 percent of those who live in the West have no religious preference.

The second general category of question answered by Type I tables is: With respect to a given social characteristic, how do the percentages in the different churched or unchurched categories compare with one another? For example, does the percentage of churched Catholics living in the Midwest differ in some way from the percentage of unchurched Catholics living in the Midwest? As indicated in the sample table above, the answer is yes. A greater percentage of churched than unchurched Catholics live in the Midwest (31 percent vs. 22 percent).

---

18. Major differences from item to item in the reported number of respondents (N) for any specific churched-unchurched type are a result of the varying number of surveys in which the items appeared. Minor differences are a result of varying numbers of "no answers" or "don't know."

19. To calculate, for example, the percentage of those who live in the West who have no religious preference one would: (1) multiply the percent of each churched-unchurched type living in the West as indicated in the table by the indicated (N) for that type; (2) sum the five figures obtained in step 1; (3) divide the figure obtained in step 1 for those expressing no religious preference by the sum obtained in step 2. For the data reported in Figure 1: $(.30 \times 507)/(.13 \times 3365)+(.22 \times 1468)+(.15 \times 1450)+(.21 \times 476)+(.30 \times 507)=12.4$ percent.

This type of question, of course, illustrates the comparative potential of our profile, and allows us to see if, and how, the various churched-unchurched types differ from one another. Although numerous comparisons between categories are possible, the following seem of most interest: (1) churched Protestants vs. unchurched Protestants vs. no religious preference; (2) churched Catholics vs. unchurched Catholics vs. no religious preference; (3) unchurched Protestants vs. unchurched Catholics vs. no religious preference; (4) churched Protestants vs. churched Catholics; and (5) the unchurched as a total group (unchurched Protestants, unchurched Catholics, and no religious preference) vs. the churched as a total group (churched Protestants and churched Catholics).

An example of the second type of table format found in the profile is as follows:

FORMAT FOR TYPE II TABLE: SAMPLE

ORGANIZATIONAL MEMBERSHIPS OF THE CHURCHED AND UNCHURCHED

	PROTESTANTS		CATHOLICS		NO RELIGIOUS PREFERENCE
	Churched	Unchurched	Churched	Unchurched	
Fraternal	15	12	12	5	8
Service	11	7	7	3	6
Labor Union	13	19	20	20	15
Church Group	65	10	42	7	4
(N)	(1306)	(581)	(543)	(190)	(210)

Type II is similar to Type I in almost every respect, and in fact, is read and used in much the same manner. The only difference is that Type I tables present data for one question with multiple response categories. Type II tables present data for one response category for a variety of distinct questions. The data presented in the Type II sample, for instance, come from four distinct questions: Do you belong to a fraternal organization--yes/no? Do you belong to a service organization--yes/no? Etc. However, only the percent answering "yes" is reported for each item. Note that in Type II tables the column percentages do not necessarily sum to 100 percent, and that the reported N is the average number of respondents answering any given question.[20]

---

20. Because of "no answers" and "don't knows," the number of respondents in Type II tables may vary from question to question. Such variation is slight, seldom being more than two or three respondents. The use of the reported average (N) will not significantly alter estimates of sampling error or recalculation of percentages.

2. Where the Churched and Unchurched Came From: Childhood Background

All information contained in the profile comes from interviews with adults, and most of it deals with the current status or attitudes of these adults. Yet we all know that to some extent one's adult status, beliefs, and attitudes are influenced by one's pre-adult experience, by where one "came from" as a child. A number of questions specifically asking about one's childhood situation were included in the surveys we have used. These questions are reported in this section.

Generally, the data indicate that the unchurched (regardless of specific category) are more likely than the churched to have been raised in the West; raised in large cities or suburbs of large cities; and raised in broken families.

Somewhat surprisingly, the data indicate little or no difference between churched and unchurched Protestants, and between churched and unchurched Catholics in family income, father's occupation, or parents' education. However, in comparison to churched and unchurched Protestants and Catholics, those expressing no religious preference are much more likely to have come from above average income families, to have come from professional and business families, and to have had more highly educated parents.

It is also of interest to note that while 93 percent of unchurched Protestants were raised in Protestant homes and 91 percent of unchurched Catholics were raised in Catholic homes, only 14 percent of those expressing no religious preference were raised in no preference homes. Eighty percent of those currently expressing no religious preference were raised in either Protestant or Catholic homes.

TABLE 1

CHILDHOOD BACKGROUND OF THE CHURCHED AND UNCHURCHED

	PROTESTANTS		CATHOLICS		NO RELIGIOUS PREFERENCE
	Churched	Unchurched	Churched	Unchurched	
REGION OF RESIDENCE AT AGE 16					
Northeast	12	16	37	43	26
Midwest	29	32	33	22	27
South	49	35	14	13	21
West	8	15	10	16	23
Foreign Country	2	2	7	6	3
(N)	(3365)	(1465)	(1450)	(476)	(507)
CITY SIZE AT AGE 16					
Rural	44	37	20	15	21
2,500 to 49,000	31	31	32	25	28
50,000 to 250,000	10	12	15	18	17
Over 250,000	10	13	25	31	21
Suburb of City over 250,000	5	7	8	11	13
(N)	(3360)	(1465)	(1449)	(476)	(505)
FAMILY SITUATION AT AGE 16					
Living with Both Parents	76	73	82	72	71
Living with Parent and Stepparent	6	6	3	5	7
Living with One Parent	11	14	11	14	15
Not Living with Either Parent	7	7	4	8	7
(N)	(3363)	(1466)	(1450)	(475)	(507)
FAMILY INCOME AT AGE 16					
Far Below Average	7	7	6	5	6
Below Average	26	24	24	22	24
Average	55	54	57	57	47
Above Average	12	15	13	16	22
(N)	(3334)	(1453)	(1433)	(470)	(497)

	PROTESTANTS		CATHOLICS		NO RELIGIOUS PREFERENCE
	Churched	Unchurched	Churched	Unchurched	
FATHER'S OCCUPATION[1]					
Professional and Business	17	18	18	18	32
Clerical and Sales	6	6	8	12	9
Service	3	4	6	7	4
Manual Workers	40	49	53	52	42
Farm	34	23	14	10	12
(N)	(2930)	(1248)	(1292)	(389)	(411)
FATHER'S EDUCATION[2]					
Less Than High School Graduate	74	71	72	71	56
High School Graduate	20	23	23	24	31
At Least Some College	6	6	5	5	13
(N)	(2917)	(1230)	(1277)	(405)	(449)
MOTHER'S EDUCATION[3]					
Less Than High School Graduate	67	63	66	65	46
High School Graduate	28	32	31	32	45
At Least Some College	5	5	3	3	9
(N)	(2961)	(1275)	(1298)	(424)	(461)
RELIGION IN WHICH RAISED					
Protestant	94	93	9	8	52
Catholic	4	3	89	91	28
Other	*	*	*	*	6
None	2	3	1	1	14
(N)	(2630)	(1175)	(1109)	(407)	(419)

*Less than one percent

1. Includes only those respondents who had working fathers
2. Includes only those respondents who remembered their fathers
3. Includes only those respondents who remembered their mothers

3. Present Status of Churched and Unchurched: Social Locations

For better or worse we all find ourselves enmeshed in a variety of socially defined groups that influence our behaviors, beliefs, and attitudes, our exposure to problems, and our command of resources. These groups may be as diverse, un-organized, and unintentional as one's birth cohort, region of residence, or social class. Or they may be groups as purposive and organized as a labor union, a church, or a political party. That the influence of these groups over one's life chances and life styles is pervasive seems unquestionable. What is questionable, however, is the accuracy of our understanding of these influences, and if accurate, our under-standing of those dimensions of our life experience where the group influences are relevant. For present purposes, these two questions might translate as: How accurate is our understanding of who the churched and unchurched are? And, what social characteristics are relevant to distinguishing the churched from the unchurched? The surveys we have used contain an unusually large number of items that allow us to pursue these questions of social location. These items are presented in this section under three subheadings: demographic characteristics; organizational memberships; and sociability.

DEMOGRAPHIC CHARACTERISTICS

Probably to no one's surprise, our data indicate that the unchurched (regardless of specific category) are more likely than the churched to be male; to be under 35 -- although age appears to have a considerably greater effect among Catholics than among

Protestants, and an even greater effect on those expressing no religious preference; to be single--undoubtedly related to the fact that they are younger; to have fewer children--undoubtedly related to the fact that they are younger and less likely to be married; to live in the West; and to perceive themselves as politically liberal--especially true of those expressing no religious preference. More surprisingly, the data indicate negligible rural-urban differences between the churched and the unchurched--except that those expressing no religious preference tend to be slightly more urban than anyone else; only very slight mobility differences between the churched and the unchurched--the unchurched seem just a bit less "rooted" than the churched; and that ethnic, social class, and "age of children" differences are not generalizable across all of our churched and unchurched categories.

With regard to ethnic comparisons between the churched and the unchurched, a significant difference between white and non-white appears only for Protestants. A greater percent of unchurched than churched Protestants are white. Among white ethnic groups, however, significant churched-unchurched differences appear only for Catholics, and then only for three specific groups: Italians--who are disproportionately unchurched, and Irish and Polish--who are disproportionately churched. It is also of interest to note that the white ethnic composition of those expressing no religious preference more closely resembles that of Protestants (heavily English and German) than of Catholics (heavily Irish, Italian, and Spanish).

Possible social class differences between the churched and the unchurched have long been a subject of dispute. Some have viewed the Church as a haven for the socially dispossessed, seeking in the church the comfort, support, and rewards otherwise denied them. Others have viewed the Church as the primary carrier of the social status quo, drawing to itself those with the greatest stake in the maintenance of that status quo, and alienating from itself those with the least commitment to it (for example, the disestablished proletariat and the upper status counter-culturalists). Such an oversimplified caricature of these opposing positions does injustice to the subtleties and dynamics of the respective arguments. Nevertheless, they suggest a provocative set of lenses through which one might filter our findings for social class. These findings are framed within the four different traditional measures of social class contained in the profile: education; occupation of head of household; family income; and self-ascribed social class identification.

Our data indicate that educational differences between churched and unchurched Protestants are extremely small, with the churched showing a slight tendency to be more highly educated. For Catholics, however, educational differences between the churched and unchurched are more pronounced, with the churched showing a distinct tendency to be more highly educated. Those expressing no religious preference are clearly more educated than any of our other four types. The percentage of persons with at least some college education is nearly double that of the next highest type.

Occupational differences between the churched and unchurched tend to follow the pattern of educational differences. Among Protestants, the churched are more likely than the unchurched to fall into the three white collar occupational categories. Among the Catholics, the churched are more likely to fall into the top two of the three white collar occupational categories. Those expressing no religious preference clearly are much more likely than any of the other four types to be in business or professional occupations.

Somewhat surprisingly, the educational and occupational differences we have found between the churched and unchurched do not hold for income. In fact, with a very slight tendency for those expressing no religious preference to fall into our upper income category, income differences between the five churched and unchurched categories are negligible.

Looking at self-appraised social class we again find a tendency among Protestants and Catholics for the churched to identify to a greater extent than the unchurched with the upper and middle classes. Somewhat surprisingly given their educational, occupational, and slight income advantages, those expressing no religious preference are no more likely to identify themselves with the middle or upper classes than any other type.

What can we conclude about social class differences between the churched and unchurched? It seems clear that social class effects cut differently for those who identify themselves as either Protestants or Catholics, than for those who express no religious preference. For the former group, there is a slight tendency for the unchurched to be of lower social status than the churched. However, in comparing either churched Protestants or churched Catholics to those expressing no religious preference, we find a clear tendency for the latter group to be of higher status.

The so-called "child-rearing" theory of religious participation holds that church involvement should be particularly great for adults during the parenting stage of their life cycle. Parents, so the theory goes, want their children to have a "religious" upbringing. Accordingly, they turn to a religious institution to fill this need, first involving their children in the life of a Church, and then involving themselves, either because it is convenient (they have to be at the church anyway to pick up and drop off their children) and/or because they want to set a good example. Empirically, the "child-rearing" effect on religious participation has not been found to be as strong as the theory implies. Past research has shown it to be limited mainly to Protestants, and to parents of school-age children. In fact, the presence of pre-school children has been found actually to decrease a family's church involvement.

What does our profile indicate? For Protestants, it shows that "age of children" differences between the churched and unchurched, although consistent with past findings, are so small as to be insignificant. Second, it shows, contrary to previous studies, that "age of children" differences between churched and unchurched Catholics are present. Unchurched Catholics are more likely than churched Catholics to have children under six years old; and less likely to have children of school age. Those expressing no religious preference are least likely of anyone to have children of school age.

TABLE 2

DEMOGRAPHIC CHARACTERISTICS OF THE CHURCHED AND UNCHURCHED

	PROTESTANTS		CATHOLICS		NO RELIGIOUS PREFERENCE
	Churched	Unchurched	Churched	Unchurched	
GENDER					
Male	42	53	45	52	63
Female	58	47	55	48	37
(N)	(3365)	(1468)	(1450)	(476)	(507)
RACE					
White	81	90	96	94	91
Non-White	19	10	4	6	9
(N)	(3365)	(1468)	(1450)	(476)	(507)
ETHNICITY					
English	16	17	3	4	13
French	2	1	3	4	2
German	17	18	13	8	14
Irish	8	9	15	13	9
Italian	1	1	14	22	5
Spanish Speaking	1	1	9	10	3
Polish	*	*	10	4	2
Slavic	1	1	6	4	6
Scottish	3	4	1	1	3
Mixed, Other	51	47	28	30	44
(N)	(3350)	(1459)	(1443)	(476)	(502)
AGE					
18 - 24	11	14	14	19	28
25 - 34	19	23	22	33	32
35 - 54	34	32	37	29	24
55 and Over	37	32	28	19	16
(N)	(3365)	(1468)	(1450)	(476)	(507)

*Less than 1 percent

	PROTESTANTS		CATHOLICS		NO RELIGIOUS PREFERENCE
	Churched	Unchurched	Churched	Unchurched	
REGION					
Northeast	13	17	38	43	24
Midwest	29	30	31	22	26
South	45	32	17	13	19
West	13	22	15	21	30
(N)	(3365)	(1468)	(1450)	(476)	(507)
CITY SIZE					
12 Largest Cities	7	9	15	19	20
Remainder of 100 Largest Cities	17	16	15	17	22
Suburbs of 12 Largest Cities	6	8	14	13	10
Suburbs of the Remaining 100 Largest Cities	7	9	10	12	7
Other Urban	42	40	37	33	31
Other Rural	20	17	10	6	9
(N)	(3365)	(1468)	(1450)	(476)	(507)
CURRENT PLACE OF RESIDENCE					
Same State and Same Area as When 16	43	39	48	44	45
Same State but Different Area Than When 16	24	27	22	29	20
Different State Than When 16	33	34	30	27	35
(N)	(3269)	(1442)	(1408)	(468)	(501)
MARITAL STATUS					
Married	72	70	72	66	51
Divorced or Separated	8	9	5	12	12
Widowed	11	8	9	6	4
Single	9	13	14	15	33
(N)	(3365)	(1468)	(1450)	(476)	(507)

	PROTESTANTS		CATHOLICS		NO RELIGIOUS PREFERENCE
	Churched	Unchurched	Churched	Unchurched	
NUMBER OF CHILDREN					
None	20	24	25	29	46
One	15	16	13	19	15
Two	24	22	20	22	15
Three	17	15	17	11	13
Four or More	23	23	25	19	11
(N)	(3347)	(1464)	(1449)	(474)	(506)
CHILD UNDER 6 LIVING IN HOUSEHOLD	22	23	26	31	23
(N)	(3365)	(1468)	(1450)	(476)	(507)
CHILD 6 - 12 LIVING IN HOUSEHOLD	26	24	32	27	21
(N)	(3365)	(1468)	(1450)	(476)	(507)
CHILD 13 - 18 LIVING IN HOUSEHOLD	24	22	29	20	19
(N)	(3365)	(1468)	(1450)	(476)	(507)
SELF-APPRAISED SOCIAL CLASS					
Lower	5	6	4	5	5
Working	46	51	46	51	45
Middle	46	41	49	43	46
Upper	3	2	1	1	3
(N)	(3347)	(1453)	(1449)	(474)	(504)
EDUCATION					
Less Than High School Graduate	39	42	32	42	26
High School Graduate	47	48	53	50	46
At Least Some College	14	10	15	8	28
(N)	(3342)	(1459)	(1443)	(476)	(504)

	PROTESTANTS		CATHOLICS		NO RELIGIOUS PREFERENCE
	Churched	Unchurched	Churched	Unchurched	
FAMILY INCOME					
Under $6,000	30	28	20	24	27
$6,000 - 9,999	21	21	20	20	19
$10,000 - 14,999	24	22	29	25	19
$15,000 - 19,999	12	14	14	17	15
$20,000 and Over	13	14	17	14	19
(N)	(3115)	(1375)	(1354)	(441)	(466)
EVER RECEIVED GOVERNMENT AID (Welfare, etc.)					
Yes	31	38	31	43	37
(N)	(2628)	(1175)	(1108)	(408)	(422)
OCCUPATION					
Professional and Business	21	19	21	17	31
Clerical and Sales	22	20	30	22	20
Service	15	13	11	16	9
Manual Worker	27	36	28	37	28
Farm	4	3	2	*	2
Not in Labor Force	11	10	8	8	10
(N)	(3365)	(1468)	(1450)	(476)	(507)
UNEMPLOYED AND LOOKING FOR WORK FOR AS LONG AS A MONTH IN THE LAST 10 YEARS					
Yes	23	30	25	37	40
(N)	(2620)	(1173)	(1108)	(406)	(424)
POLITICAL PARTY					
Democratic	42	43	52	46	32
Independent	29	34	33	42	56
Republican	30	23	15	13	12
(N)	(3258)	(1411)	(1410)	(457)	(470)

*Less than 1 percent

	PROTESTANTS		CATHOLICS		NO RELIGIOUS PREFERENCE
	Churched	Unchurched	Churched	Unchurched	
SELF-APPRAISED POLITICAL ORIENTATION					
Liberal	24	30	27	34	56
Moderate	40	43	43	45	25
Conservative	36	27	30	21	19
(N)	(1844)	(839)	(792)	(287)	(311)
NEWSPAPER READING					
Everyday	67	65	75	63	51
A Few Times a Week	15	15	15	15	21
Once a Week or Less	18	20	10	22	28
(N)	(1425)	(574)	(594)	(177)	(196)
EVER BEEN PICKED UP BY POLICE FOR ANY REASON WHETHER OR NOT YOU WERE GUILTY?					
Yes	7	12	6	19	26
(N)	(1895)	(865)	(844)	(290)	(306)

ORGANIZATIONAL MEMBERSHIPS

The data reported in this section were obtained in response to the following question:

> We would like to know something about the groups
> and organizations to which individuals belong. Here
> is a list of various kinds of organizations. Could
> you tell me whether or not you are a member of each?

Generally the data show that the unchurched (regardless of specific type) are not only not involved in the life of the Church, but are also less likely than the churched to be involved in any type of organization. The exceptions to this general pattern include unchurched Protestants' slight tendency to be more involved than churched Protestants in veterans' organizations and labor unions; the equal or nearly equal liklihood of churched and unchurched Catholics to be involved in labor unions and sports organizations; and the tendency for those expressing no religious preference to be just as involved as anyone else in political organizations, sports organizations,

"literary, discussion, or study groups" and "professional or academic societies."
The exceptional organizational membership pattern of those expressing no religious
preference is undoubtedly related to their distinct age, educational, and occupational
characteristics, which we have discussed in the previous section.

TABLE 3

ORGANIZATIONAL MEMBERSHIPS OF THE CHURCHED AND UNCHURCHED

	PROTESTANTS		CATHOLICS		NO RELIGIOUS PREFERENCE
	Churched	Unchurched	Churched	Unchurched	
Fraternal	15	12	12	5	8
Service	11	7	7	3	6
Veterans'	8	9	12	7	6
Political	5	3	5	2	5
Labor Union	13	19	20	20	15
Sports	18	17	22	20	21
Youth Group	13	6	10	3	10
School Service Group	20	8	19	7	8
Hobby or Garden Club	11	7	10	7	8
Nationality Group	3	1	5	2	1
Literary, Discussion or Study	11	5	9	3	13
Professional or Academic Society	14	8	14	9	14
Church-Affiliated Group	65	10	42	7	4
(N)	(1306)	(581)	(543)	(190)	(210)

SOCIABILITY

Sociability refers to those types of persons with whom one associates for the
sheer enjoyment of their company, without thought of more practical or serious purposes. As a means of obtaining information on sociability, the surveys ask a number
of questions regarding how one is likely to spend a "social evening." These questions
are reported in this section.

Generally, the data indicate that the unchurched (regardless of specific type) are
slightly less likely than the churched to spend a social evening with relatives, and
more likely to spend a social evening at a bar or tavern. Differences are especially
great for those expressing no religious preference. The data also indicate that those
expressing no religious preference are more likely than anyone else to spend a social
evening with friends who live outside of their immediate neighborhood.

TABLE 4

SOCIABILITY OF THE CHURCHED AND UNCHURCHED

	PROTESTANTS		CATHOLICS		NO RELIGIOUS PREFERENCE
	Churched	Unchurched	Churched	Unchurched	
PERCENT SPENDING AT LEAST ONE EVENING A WEEK...					
Socializing with Relatives	41	35	40	37	31
Socializing with Someone who Lives in the Neighborhood	31	27	29	29	29
Socializing with Friends who Live Outside of the Neighborhood	20	20	23	24	32
At a Bar or Tavern	6	14	11	16	25
(N)	(1314)	(586)	(544)	(189)	(211)

4. Religious Characteristics of the Churched and Unchurched

To say that someone is "churched," as we have defined the term, does not necessarily imply that that person is highly commited to the Church, nor that that person necessarily holds a positive image of the Church, nor even that that person necessarily holds certain beliefs. Conversely, to say that someone is "unchurched," as we have defined the term, does not necessarily imply that that person does not take his or her religion seriously, nor that that person necessarily holds a negative image of the Church, nor even that that person is a "non-believer." The data reported in this section provide some insight into the frequency with which such apparent incongruities occur, as well as providing some indication of the extent to which other predisposing religious factors (such as the religion in which one was raised, or one's spouse's religious preference) affect one's current status of being either churched or unchurched.

As previously noted, our data show that churched and unchurched Protestants are equally likely to have been raised as Protestants. Similarly, the data show that churched and unchurched Catholics are equally likely to have been raised as Catholics. For those currently expressing no religious preference, however, the data present an entirely different pattern. Only a relatively few (14 percent) were raised with no religious preference, the vast majority being raised as either Protestants (52 percent) or Catholics (28 percent).

In our five-fold categorization of the churched and unchurched, we have grouped all Protestants together. But one might rightly wonder to what extent the various Protestant denominations differ in their respective proportions of churched and unchurched. Looking only at Protestants, the data show that the unchurched are less likely to be Baptists or Lutherans, and more likely to be Methodists, Presbyterians, Episcopalians, or "other" Protestants. With the exception of the Baptists, however, the differences are very slight.

Past research has shown that the religious participation of persons from mixed religious marriages is lower than that of those from marriages in which both spouses have the same religious preference. Our data support this previous finding. For both Protestants and Catholics, the unchurched are considerably more likely to be involved in mixed religious marriages than the churched. The effect is especially strong for Catholics.

To what extent is the self-perceived saliency of one's commitment to a religious tradition related to one's involvement in the institutionalized life of that tradition? As might be expected, our data show the relationship to be quite strong. Churched Protestants and Catholics are much more likely than their unchurched counterparts to identify themselves as strong or very strong Protestants or Catholics. Nevertheless, the relationship is far from perfect. In fact, a full third of both churched Protestants and churched Catholics do not feel they are strong or very strong Protestants or Catholics; and one in five unchurched Protestants and unchurched Catholics identify themselves as either strong or very strong Protestants or Catholics.

Unfortunately, our surveys contain only one question dealing with religious belief, and it is a rather simplistic question at that: "Do you believe in life after death?" Nevertheless, the results are interesting. Eighty-two percent of churched Protestants and 74 percent of churched Catholics said they believe in life after death. The respective percentages for unchurched Protestants and unchurched Catholics are 60 percent and 53 percent. These are, of course, significantly lower than those for their churched counterparts. But, in each case, believers still outnumber non-believers. For those expressing no religious preference, only 41 percent said that they believe in life after death.

To what extent do our five churched and unchurched categories differ in regard to their confidence in religious leaders? Not surprisingly, our data show that sizeable differences exist, but in no case is the percentage expressing a great deal of confidence in religious leaders greater than 50 percent. Churched Catholics are more likely than any of our other categories to express a great deal of confidence in religious leaders. Churched Protestants are next most likely, followed by unchurched Protestants and Catholics. Those expressing no religious preference are least likely to express a great deal of confidence in religious leaders.

TABLE 5

RELIGIOUS CHARACTERISTICS OF THE CHURCHED AND UNCHURCHED

	PROTESTANTS		CATHOLICS		NO RELIGIOUS PREFERENCE
	Churched	Unchurched	Churched	Unchurched	
RELIGION IN WHICH RAISED					
Protestant	94	93	9	8	52
Catholic	4	3	89	91	28
Other	*	*	*	*	6
None	2	3	1	1	14
(N)	(2630)	(1175)	(1109)	(407)	(419)
CURRENT PROTESTANT PREFERENCE					
Baptist	35	27			
Methodist	19	23			
Lutheran	13	11			
Presbyterian	7	9			
Episcopalian	4	6			
Other Protestant	22	25			
(N)	(3362)	(1466)			
SPOUSE'S RELIGION					
Protestant	93	81	13	31	42
Catholic	4	13	84	56	18
Other	*	*	*	2	3
None	3	5	2	10	36
(N)	(1902)	(816)	(762)	(263)	(208)
SELF-APPRAISED SALIENCY OF RELIGIOUS IDENTIFICATION[1]					
Strong	55	13	52	8	
Somewhat Strong	13	8	13	8	
Not Very Strong	33	79	35	84	
(N)	(1959)	(861)	(820)	(298)	

*Less than one percent

1. This question was asked only of those who expressed a religious preference

	PROTESTANTS		CATHOLICS		NO RELIGIOUS PREFERENCE
	Churched	Unchurched	Churched	Unchurched	
BELIEF IN LIFE AFTER DEATH					
Yes	82	60	74	53	41
No	11	27	20	34	46
Don't Know	7	13	7	13	13
(N)	(1987)	(866)	(814)	(326)	(322)
CONFIDENCE IN RELIGIOUS LEADERS					
A Great Deal	39	25	45	25	12
Only Some	43	49	45	52	42
Hardly Any	14	21	8	20	40
Don't Know	5	6	2	3	6
(N)	(2620)	(1172)	(1104)	(405)	(421)
MEMBERSHIP IN CHURCH-AFFILIATED GROUP	65	10	42	7	4
(N)	(1325)	(582)	(540)	(189)	(210)

5. Quality of Life of the Churched and Unchurched

All too often "quality of life" is identified with material possessions and/or objective situations. This is not what is dealt with in this section. Rather, the data reported here speak to the issue of "quality of life" first from the perspective of subjective self-evaluations of one's life experience, and then from the perspective of what might be called interpersonal alienation.

Questions asked within the first perspective attempt to assess the extent to which one has been able to realize self-perceptions of the "good" life. They are phrased primarily in terms of one's self-perceived happiness or satisfaction.

Questions asked within the second perspective attempt to assess one's degree of confidence in the trustworthiness, honesty, and basic goodness of people in general and the extent of one's hopefulness or despair for the future.

SATISFACTION

With one exception, the data show churched Protestants and Catholics more likely than their unchurched counterparts to express satisfaction with or happiness in those nine life situations covered by our questions. The exception is that of personal health. In this case, churched and unchurched Catholics are equally likely to express satisfaction. The data also show that, with the exception of work and current financial situation, those expressing no religious preference are less likely than any other group to express a high degree of happiness or satisfaction. Somewhat surprising, however, is the fact that while those expressing no religious preference are least satisfied with their current life situations, they are the most likely to indicate that they find life exciting.

It is also of interest to note that regardless of specific churched-unchurched type only about one in three persons indicate that, all things considered, he/she is very happy. For specific dimensions of one's life experience, greatest satisfaction is expressed in the areas of family life and friendships.

TABLE 6

SATISFACTION IN LIFE, AS EXPERIENCED BY THE CHURCHED AND UNCHURCHED

	PROTESTANTS		CATHOLICS		NO RELIGIOUS PREFERENCE
	Churched	Unchurched	Churched	Unchurched	
TAKEN ALL TOGETHER, HOW HAPPY WOULD YOU SAY YOU ARE?					
Very Happy	39	31	34	28	23
Pretty Happy	50	52	53	56	61
Not Too Happy	11	17	14	16	16
(N)	(3358)	(1468)	(1445)	(476)	(502)
IN GENERAL, DO YOU FIND LIFE:					
Exciting	47	40	42	42	52
Routine	50	54	54	52	42
Dull	3	6	4	6	6
(N)	(1900)	(872)	(843)	(293)	(307)
TAKING THINGS ALL TOGETHER, WOULD YOU DESCRIBE YOUR MARRIAGE AS:[1]					
Very Happy	71	61	71	67	56
Pretty Happy	27	35	27	30	39
Not Too Happy	2	4	2	3	5
(N)	(1898)	(817)	(759)	(263)	(211)

1. Asked of married persons only

| | PROTESTANTS | | CATHOLICS | | NO RELIGIOUS PREFERENCE |
	Churched	Unchurched	Churched	Unchurched	
ON THE WHOLE, HOW SATISFIED ARE YOU WITH THE WORK YOU DO?[2]					
Very Satisfied	54	48	52	42	45
Moderately Satisfied	34	38	36	38	34
A Little Dissatisfied	8	10	9	14	13
Very Dissatisfied	3	5	3	6	8
(N)	(2461)	(1088)	(1105)	(385)	(375)
HOW SATISFIED ARE YOU WITH YOUR FAMILY'S PRESENT FINANCIAL SITUATION?					
Pretty Well Satisfied	35	30	28	25	28
More or Less Satisfied	44	44	49	45	42
Not Satisfied at All	21	26	23	30	30
(N)	(3352)	(1463)	(1445)	(476)	(505)
DURING THE LAST FEW YEARS HAS YOUR FINANCIAL SITUATION CHANGED?					
Getting Better	40	38	38	40	41
Getting Worse	20	23	22	24	22
Stayed the Same	40	39	40	36	37
(N)	(3333)	(1450)	(1429)	(469)	(502)
PERSONS INDICATING A GREAT DEAL OF SATISFACTION WITH:					
The City or Place They Live	55	43	49	43	31
Non-Working Activities	59	53	54	52	53
Family Life	80	72	79	74	58
Friendships	76	65	71	66	59
Health and Physical Condition	62	56	63	63	55
(N)	(2625)	(1172)	(1106)	(406)	(422)

2. Asked only of those employed

ANOMIE AND MISANTHROPY

The data reported in this section deal with one's perception of the trustworthiness, honesty, and goodness of people in general and of one's hopefulness or despair for the future.

The data show that the unchurched are more likely than the churched to be characterized by misanthropy, normlessness and despair. Differences for Protestants, although consistent, are relatively small. For Catholics, however, the differences are quite substantial. Where those expressing no religious preference stand in comparison to churched and unchurched Protestants and Catholics varies considerably from item to item and defies easy summation.

TABLE 7

ANOMIE, AS EXPERIENCED BY THE CHURCHED AND UNCHURCHED

	PROTESTANTS		CATHOLICS		NO RELIGIOUS PREFERENCE
	Churched	Unchurched	Churched	Unchurched	
PERCENT AGREEING					
Next to Health, Money is the Most Important Thing in Life	28	33	34	38	26
You Sometimes Can't Help Wondering Whether Anything is Worthwhile Any More	39	48	40	47	42
To Make Money, There are No Right and Wrong Ways Any More, Only Easy Ways And Hard Ways	20	25	26	36	28
Nowadays, a Person has to Live Pretty Much for Today and Let Tomorrow Take Care of Itself	47	46	40	50	43
In Spite of What Some People Say, the Lot (Situation, Condition) of the Average Man is Getting Worse, not Better	58	62	56	67	56

	PROTESTANTS		CATHOLICS		NO RELIGIOUS PREFERENCE
	Churched	Unchurched	Churched	Unchurched	

PERCENT AGREEING (cont.)

It's Hardly Fair to Bring a Child into the World with the Way Things Look for the Future	39	44	30	47	38
Most Public Officials (People in Public Office) are not Really Interested in Problems of the Average Man	65	69	59	71	63
These Days a Person Doesn't Really Know Whom he Can Count on	76	77	71	78	73
Most People Don't Really Care What Happens to the Next Fellow	60	62	53	62	54
(N)	(1285)	(610)	(572)	(193)	(215)

TABLE 8

MISANTHROPY, AS MANIFESTED BY THE CHURCHED AND UNCHURCHED

	PROTESTANTS		CATHOLICS		NO RELIGIOUS PREFERENCE
	Churched	Unchurched	Churched	Unchurched	

PERCENT AGREEING

People Try to be Helpful as Opposed to Just Looking Out for Themselves	51	46	52	43	44
People Try to be Fair as Opposed to Trying to Take Advantage of You	61	56	66	55	52

	PROTESTANTS		CATHOLICS		NO RELIGIOUS PREFERENCE
	Churched	Unchurched	Churched	Unchurched	
PERCENT AGREEING (cont.)					
Most People Can be Trusted	44	42	49	41	45
(N)	(2705)	(1154)	(1152)	(393)	(404)

6. Attitudes of the Churched and Unchurched

An "attitude," as the term is used here, refers to an individual's positive or negative evaluation of a specific situation, principle, or group of persons. Social scientists believe that such an expression of opinion is generally a particularized application of more abstract values and beliefs, and that it represents a predisposition to act accordingly. For example, one's attitude toward the death penalty should provide some insight into one's fundamental understanding of justice and the sanctity of life; and it should also provide some indication as to how one might vote if the issue were presented in a public referendum.

The series of surveys upon which this profile depends contains as varied and extensive a set of attitude items as are to be found in any national data source of comparable sample size. These items are presented in this section under the following general headings:

> National issues
> Feminist issues
> Sexual issues
> Fertility, birth control, and abortion
> Attitudes toward blacks
> Attitudes toward work
> Confidence in the leadership of major American institutions
> Desirable qualities for children
> Civil liberties: atheist, socialist, communist, homosexual

NATIONAL ISSUES

This section deals with those issues of continual public debate for which our surveys have but a single attitudinal measure. Included among these issues are: wire-tapping, the death penalty, gun control, busing, divorce laws, the courts' handling of criminals, the use of marijuana, pornography, and U.S. involvement in world affairs and in the United Nations. Given such a diversity of issues, it is not altogether surprising that the attitudinal differences between our five churched and unchurched categories are summarized only at some risk. In general, it appears safe to say that with the exception of divorce and marijuana, attitudinal differences between churched and unchurched Protestants and Catholics are relatively insignificant, but those expressing no religious preference are considerably more "liberal" or "non-traditional." On divorce, both unchurched Protestants and unchurched Catholics are considerably more likely than their churched counterparts to favor making divorce easier. On the use of marijuana, both unchurched Protestants and unchurched Catholics are considerably more likely than their churched counterparts to favor legalization.

TABLE 9

ATTITUDES OF THE CHURCHED AND UNCHURCHED ABOUT NATIONAL ISSUES

	PROTESTANTS		CATHOLICS		NO RELIGIOUS PREFERENCE
	Churched	Unchurched	Churched	Unchurched	
WIRETAPPING					
In General, Approve	17	18	14	17	13
In General, Disapprove	78	78	83	81	83
No Opinion	5	4	3	3	4
(N)	(1331)	(589)	(547)	(190)	(214)
DEATH PENALTY FOR CONVICTED MURDERERS					
Favor	58	64	65	68	47
Oppose	36	30	30	29	48
Don't Know	7	6	5	3	5
(N)	(3352)	(1457)	(1447)	(474)	(507)

	PROTESTANTS		CATHOLICS		NO RELIGIOUS PREFERENCE
	Churched	Unchurched	Churched	Unchurched	
LAW REQUIRING A POLICE PERMIT TO BUY A GUN					
Favor	69	67	82	82	72
Oppose	29	31	16	17	27
Don't Know	2	2	2	1	1
(N)	(3350)	(1462)	(1446)	(476)	(505)
BUSING OF SCHOOL CHILDREN FROM ONE SCHOOL DISTRICT TO ANOTHER					
In General, Favor	19	17	17	18	31
In General, Oppose	77	80	79	79	65
Don't Know	4	3	4	3	4
(N)	(2063)	(880)	(887)	(259)	(295)
OBTAINING A DIVORCE SHOULD BE:					
Easier	24	39	24	40	63
More Difficult	55	36	54	40	21
Stay As It Is	21	25	22	20	16
(N)	(1262)	(566)	(522)	(179)	(204)
COURTS HANDLING OF CRIMINALS					
Too Harsh	4	5	3	8	12
Not Harsh Enough	76	75	75	72	56
About Right	11	11	12	12	14
Don't Know	9	10	10	9	18
(N)	(3355)	(1456)	(1442)	(474)	(500)
THE USE OF MARIJUANA SHOULD BE:					
Legal	14	25	21	31	53
Illegal	84	70	76	65	42
Don't Know	2	5	3	4	5
(N)	(1986)	(864)	(811)	(325)	(323)

	PROTESTANTS		CATHOLICS		NO RELIGIOUS PREFERENCE
	Churched	Unchurched	Churched	Unchurched	
PORNOGRAPHY: THERE SHOULD BE:					
Laws Against Its Distribution to Anyone	50	34	46	27	17
Laws Against Its Distribution to Persons Under 18	43	56	47	64	58
No Laws Against Its Distribution	7	10	6	9	25
(N)	(1942)	(853)	(804)	(321)	(315)
UNITED NATIONS: U.S. SHOULD:					
Continue to Belong	73	73	80	80	78
Pull Out Now	19	20	15	14	15
Don't Know	8	7	5	6	8
(N)	(1985)	(863)	(810)	(326)	(323)
ROLE OF U.S. IN WORLD AFFAIRS					
Should be Active	60	60	59	53	61
Should Stay Out	36	36	37	44	35
Don't Know	5	4	4	3	4
(N)	(1652)	(711)	(668)	(261)	(261)

FEMINIST ISSUES

The feminist movement in the United States is a complex intertwining of a variety of opinions on a variety of issues. The three questions for which we present data in this section certainly cannot begin to do justice to the subtleties that are involved. Nevertheless, each question seems to touch on a pivotal concern, and in that sense can provide a rough gauge of how our five churched and unchurched categories might look on the deeper issues.

The data indicate that while differences between churched and unchurched Protestants and Catholics are almost negligible, the unchurched consistently show a greater openness toward women moving out of traditional roles. Considerably larger differences are encountered, however, when comparing those expressing no religious preference to anyone else. Those expressing no religious preference are by far and away the most sympathetic to feminist concerns.

TABLE 10

ATTITUDES OF THE CHURCHED AND UNCHURCHED ABOUT FEMINIST ISSUES

	PROTESTANTS		CATHOLICS		NO RELIGIOUS PREFERENCE
	Churched	Unchurched	Churched	Unchurched	
WOMEN SHOULD TAKE CARE OF RUNNING THEIR HOMES AND LEAVE RUNNING THE COUNTRY UP TO MEN	40	37	29	30	16
(N)	(1331)	(592)	(548)	(190)	(214)
DISAPPROVE OF A MARRIED WOMAN EARNING MONEY IN BUSINESS OR INDUSTRY IF SHE HAS A HUSBAND CAPABLE OF SUPPORTING HER	33	30	33	30	18
(N)	(2059)	(882)	(888)	(259)	(297)
WOULD NOT VOTE FOR A WOMAN FOR PRESIDENT, IF MY PARTY NOMINATED HER	25	21	19	15	11
(N)	(2066)	(882)	(886)	(259)	(297)

SEXUAL ISSUES

The data reported in this section deal with sex education; pre-marital, extra-marital, and homosexual relations; and a variety of attitudes regarding pornography. It shows that the percentage favoring sex education in the public schools differs significantly in each of our five churched and unchurched categories. Those expressing no religious preference are most favorable, followed in decreasing order by unchurched Catholics, churched Catholics, unchurched Protestants, and churched Protestants, who are least favorable. It also shows that large differences exist between the attitudes of the churched and the unchurched (regardless of specific category) toward pre-marital, extra-marital, and homosexual sexual relations. In each case, churched Protestants are most likely to indicate that the relationship is wrong, followed in decreasing order by churched Catholics, unchurched Protestants, unchurched Catholics, and those expressing no religious preference, who are the least likely by a considerable margin. These differences in sexual attitudes among our five churched and unchurched categories are as large as any encountered in the profile, including those found in regard to belief in life after death. Finally, in general the unchurched (regardless of specific type, but especially for those expressing no religious preference) are more favorable in their attitudes toward pornography than the churched.

TABLE 11

ATTITUDES OF THE CHURCHED AND UNCHURCHED ABOUT SEXUAL ISSUES

	PROTESTANTS		CATHOLICS		NO RELIGIOUS PREFERENCE
	Churched	Unchurched	Churched	Unchurched	
FAVOR SEX EDUCATION IN THE PUBLIC SCHOOLS	76	82	84	85	92
(N)	(1279)	(567)	(524)	(183)	(209)
IF A MAN AND WOMAN HAVE SEXUAL RELATIONS BEFORE MARRIAGE, IT IS:					
Always Wrong	42	22	36	14	7
Almost Always Wrong	14	12	13	9	2
Wrong Only Sometimes	20	27	25	23	22
Not Wrong at All	20	35	23	50	64
Don't Know	4	4	3	4	3
(N)	(2060)	(880)	(885)	(258)	(295)
IF A MARRIED PERSON HAS SEXUAL RELATIONS WITH SOMEONE OTHER THAN THE MARRIAGE PARTNER, IT IS:					
Always Wrong	79	66	75	60	35
Almost Always Wrong	11	16	13	15	19
Wrong Only Sometimes	7	13	10	17	30
Not Wrong at All	2	3	2	7	14
Don't Know	1	2	*	1	2
(N)	(1934)	(891)	(856)	(297)	(311)

*Less than 1 percent

	PROTESTANTS		CATHOLICS		NO RELIGIOUS PREFERENCE
	Churched	Unchurched	Churched	Unchurched	
SEXUAL RELATIONS BETWEEN TWO ADULTS OF THE SAME SEX IS:					
Always Wrong	78	66	69	58	35
Almost Always Wrong	4	6	7	8	7
Wrong Only Sometimes	5	8	7	11	15
Not Wrong at All	7	14	11	18	34
Don't Know	6	6	5	5	9
(N)	(1929)	(891)	(855)	(297)	(310)
PORNOGRAPHY PROVIDES INFORMATION ABOUT SEX					
Yes	58	64	56	63	72
No	33	30	38	30	22
Don't Know	9	6	5	7	5
(N)	(1981)	(864)	(811)	(326)	(323)
PORNOGRAPHY LEADS TO A BREAKDOWN OF MORALS					
Yes	61	48	60	40	23
No	31	45	35	53	71
Don't Know	8	7	5	7	6
(N)	(1981)	(865)	(811)	(326)	(322)
PORNOGRAPHY LEADS PEOPLE TO COMMIT RAPE					
Yes	59	47	56	45	23
No	31	45	37	46	71
Don't Know	10	8	7	9	6
(N)	(1978)	(861)	(811)	(326)	(323)

	PROTESTANTS		CATHOLICS		NO RELIGIOUS PREFERENCE
	Churched	Unchurched	Churched	Unchurched	

PORNOGRAPHY PROVIDES AN
OUTLET FOR BOTTLED-UP
IMPULSES

Yes	54	53	59	58	61
No	30	32	30	31	29
Don't Know	16	14	11	11	10
(N)	(1979)	(862)	(812)	(326)	(323)

FERTILITY, BIRTH CONTROL, ABORTION

Old stereotypes and recent events suggest that a comparison of churched and unchurched Protestants and Catholics on the subject of fertility, birth control and abortion should yield rather substantial differences. The data reported in this section do not disappoint such expectations.

In response to a question concerning the ideal number of children for a family to have, our data indicate that churched Catholics are more likely than any of our other churched-unchurched types to idealize a family of three or more children; that unchurched Catholics are considerably less likely than their churched counterparts to idealize a family of three or more children, less so even than churched Protestants; and that unchurched Protestants and those expressing no religious preference are slightly less likely than unchurched Catholics to idealize a large family.

On the subject of birth control, the two items for which we have data are, unfortunately, extremely general in wording. They ask only whether or not "birth control information" should be available to any adult who wants it, and whether or not it should be available to teenagers who want it. The most distinguishing characteristic of the data in regard to the first question is the almost universal agreement (90 percent or more for all five of our churched and unchurched categories) that birth control information should be available to any adult who wants it. There are no significant Catholic-Protestant differences, and there is only a very slight tendency for the unchurched to be more supportive of the dissemination of birth control information than the churched.

In turning to the second question, the data indicate that the dissemination of birth control information to teenagers who want it is less generally acceptable than its dissemination to adults who want it. We also find that while differences among our churched and unchurched categories on this second question follow the same general pattern as for the first question, they are more distinct.

On the subject of abortion, persons were asked whether or not an abortion should be legal in each of six different situations. Regardless of specific situation, churched Catholics were always the least likely of our five churched and unchurched categories to feel abortion should be legal; after churched Catholics, churched Protestants were next least likely to feel abortion should be legal; there were no significant differences between unchurched Protestants and unchurched Catholics, both groups considerably more likely to be pro-abortion than either churched Protestants or churched Catholics; and those expressing no religious preference were most likely of our five types to be pro-abortion. These differences were particularly large in those situations which did not involve a possible defect in the baby, danger to the health of the mother, or rape.

TABLE 12

ATTITUDES OF THE CHURCHED AND UNCHURCHED ABOUT FERTILITY,
BIRTH CONTROL AND ABORTION

	PROTESTANTS		CATHOLICS		NO RELIGIOUS PREFERENCE
	Churched	Unchurched	Churched	Unchurched	
IDEAL NUMBER OF CHILDREN FOR A FAMILY					
None	1	2	1	1	4
One	1	2	1	2	3
Two	44	54	34	47	53
Three	24	21	29	28	18
Four or More	24	16	26	14	14
As Many As You Want	6	5	9	7	9
(N)	(2003)	(864)	(859)	(255)	(279)
BIRTH CONTROL INFORMATION SHOULD BE AVAILABLE TO ANYONE WHO WANTS IT	90	93	90	94	97
(N)	(1310)	(582)	(539)	(188)	(213)

	PROTESTANTS		CATHOLICS		NO RELIGIOUS PREFERENCE
	Churched	Unchurched	Churched	Unchurched	
BIRTH CONTROL INFORMATION SHOULD BE AVAILABLE TO TEENAGERS WHO WANT IT	75	81	76	84	93
(N)	(1326)	(586)	(544)	(188)	(211)
ABORTIONS SHOULD BE LEGAL IF:					
There is a Strong Chance of Serious Defect in the Baby	81	90	73	91	93
(N)	(3233)	(1431)	(1389)	(461)	(499)
Woman is Married and Does Not Want any More Children	37	53	28	56	73
(N)	(3358)	(1466)	(1466)	(475)	(507)
If Woman's Own Health is Seriously Endangered by the Pregnancy	87	93	81	95	97
(N)	(3355)	(1466)	(1444)	(475)	(507)
If Family has Very Low Income and Cannot Afford any More Children	45	61	35	61	75
(N)	(3353)	(1464)	(1443)	(475)	(507)
If Woman Became Pregnant as a Result of Rape	77	86	70	89	90
(N)	(3356)	(1464)	(1441)	(475)	(507)
If Woman is Not Married and Does Not Want to Marry the Man	40	56	32	56	73
(N)	(3356)	(1464)	(1443)	(475)	(507)

ATTITUDES TOWARD BLACKS

Considerable debate has raged regarding the Church's role in the perpetuation of racism. This debate has been fueled by a number of conflicting studies, some of which report significant associations between religious commitment and racial prejudice, and others which report that any association that might exist between religious commitment and prejudice is spurious, a consequence of prior and predisposing non-religious factors. Our data, unfortunately, shed but little light on this continuing controversy. The data indicate that while slightly more unchurched Protestants and Catholics tend to express prejudicial attitudes than their churched counterparts, those expressing no religious preference are considerably less likely to express prejudicial attitudes than either churched Protestants or churched Catholics, especially churched Protestants.

TABLE 13

ATTITUDES OF WHITE CHURCHED AND UNCHURCHED TOWARD BLACKS

	PROTESTANTS		CATHOLICS		NO RELIGIOUS PREFERENCE
	Churched	Unchurched	Churched	Unchurched	
NEGROES SHOULDN'T PUSH THEMSELVES WHERE THEY ARE NOT WANTED					
Strongly Agree	48	51	40	40	30
(N)	(2129)	(1012)	(1061)	(364)	(353)
WOULD YOU OBJECT IF A MEMBER OF YOUR FAMILY WANTED TO BRING A NEGRO FRIEND HOME TO DINNER?					
Strongly Object	15	17	8	14	8
(N)	(2153)	(1049)	(1142)	(343)	(358)
WOULD YOU VOTE FOR A NEGRO FOR PRESIDENT IF YOUR PARTY NOMINATED A QUALIFIED ONE?					
No	22	26	15	17	14
(N)	(1647)	(786)	(853)	(242)	(268)

	PROTESTANTS		CATHOLICS		NO RELIGIOUS PREFERENCE
	Churched	Unchurched	Churched	Unchurched	
WOULD YOU OBJECT TO SENDING YOUR CHILDREN TO A SCHOOL WHERE HALF OF THE CHILDREN ARE NEGROES?					
Yes	23	23	20	21	11
(N)	(1520)	(721)	(811)	(226)	(254)
THERE SHOULD BE LAWS AGAINST MARRIAGES BETWEEN NEGROES AND WHITES	46	41	26	25	17
(N)	(2722)	(1308)	(1384)	(445)	(460)

ATTITUDES TOWARD WORK

That one must work, someone has said, is as certain as the sun--the question is whether one works grudgingly or works gratefully, and to what purpose. Although the items for which data are presented in this section use "work" in a more limited sense (they generally refer only to that work for which one is paid), they nevertheless speak to the same questions. Specifically, they ask how satisfied one is with the work he or she does; whether or not one would work if it were economically possible not to; how important work is for "getting ahead"; and what quality one feels to be most preferable in a job. Generally the data show no significant differences in the distribution of churched and unchurched Protestant and Catholic answers to these questions. However, as we have often found to be the case as we have progressed through the profile, significant differences do appear when comparing those expressing no religious preference to everyone else. Generally, those expressing no religious preference are less likely than any other group to say that they are very satisfied with their work; less likely to indicate that hard work is the most important reason why people get ahead; less likely to indicate they would stop working if economically they could afford to; and less likely to list "high income" as the most preferable quality in a job. Not surprisingly, they are most likely to list "meaningfulness of job" as the most preferable quality in a job.

TABLE 14

ATTITUDES OF THE CHURCHED AND UNCHURCHED TOWARD WORK

	PROTESTANTS		CATHOLICS		NO RELIGIOUS PREFERENCE
	Churched	Unchurched	Churched	Unchurched	
SATISFACTION WITH WORK ONE DOES[1]					
Very Satisfied	54	48	52	52	45
(N)	(2461)	(1088)	(1105)	(385)	(375)
WHY DO PEOPLE GET AHEAD?					
Hard Work Is Most Important	67	65	63	59	53
Hard Work and Luck Equally Important	24	26	26	27	28
Luck Most Important	9	10	12	14	18
(N)	(1915)	(879)	(844)	(294)	(299)
IF YOU WERE TO GET ENOUGH MONEY TO LIVE AS COMFORTABLY AS YOU WOULD LIKE TO FOR THE REST OF YOUR LIFE, WOULD YOU[1]					
Continue to Work	68	66	67	66	75
Stop Working	32	34	33	34	25
(N)	(959)	(489)	(450)	(168)	(209)
MOST PREFERABLE QUALITY IN A JOB					
High Income	20	21	16	23	15
Job Security	7	8	9	9	5
Short Hours	4	5	3	5	7
Chances for Advancement	18	17	22	19	14
Meaningfulness of Job	52	49	49	43	60
(N)	(1903)	(872)	(844)	(294)	(303)

1. Asked only of those working.

CONFIDENCE IN THE LEADERSHIP OF MAJOR AMERICAN INSTITUTIONS

    We have already noted that the unchurched express considerably less confidence in the leadership of organized religion than do the churched. This section provides the occasion to ask whether such lack of confidence on the part of the unchurched is peculiar to their disaffection with religious institutions, or whether it is a part of a more general pattern of skepticism concerning the efficacy of national leadership. Data concerning expressed confidence in the leadership of 12 major American institutions is reported.

    Comparing churched and unchurched Protestants and Catholics, the data indicate that the unchurched are significantly less likely than their churched counterparts to express a great deal of confidence in the leadership of organized religion, major companies, and education. Secondly, the data indicate that the unchurched are significantly more likely than their churched counterparts to express a great deal of confidence only in the leadership of the mass media--television and the press. And finally, differences between the churched and unchurched are negligible in regard to the three branches of the federal government, organized labor, medicine, the scientific community, and the military.

    In comparison to churched and unchurched Protestants and Catholics, those expressing no religious preference tend to express less confidence in the leadership of all the institutions listed, with the exception of the press, the U.S. Supreme Court, and the scientific community. With respect to these three exceptions, no significant differences appear between those expressing no religious preference and any other group.

TABLE 15

CONFIDENCE IN THE LEADERSHIP OF MAJOR AMERICAN INSTITUTIONS
ON THE PART OF THE CHURCHED AND UNCHURCHED

	PROTESTANTS		CATHOLICS		NO RELIGIOUS PREFERENCE
	Churched	Unchurched	Churched	Unchurched	
PERCENT EXPRESSING A GREAT DEAL OF CONFIDENCE IN THE PERSONS RUNNING:					
Major Companies	27	24	28	22	22
Organized Religion	39	25	45	25	12
Education	41	37	43	35	28
Executive Branch of Federal Government	20	17	16	15	10

	PROTESTANTS		CATHOLICS		NO RELIGIOUS PREFERENCE
	Churched	Unchurched	Churched	Unchurched	

PERCENT EXPRESSING A GREAT
DEAL OF CONFIDENCE IN THE
PERSONS RUNNING (cont.)

	Churched	Unchurched	Churched	Unchurched	
Organized Labor	13	15	16	19	10
Press	22	30	26	30	26
Medicine	56	58	55	54	47
Television	18	23	20	22	14
U.S. Supreme Court	32	35	33	35	32
Scientific Community	37	40	45	46	45
Congress	17	15	20	20	10
Military	38	39	38	40	21
(N)	(2625)	(1169)	(1106)	(407)	(423)

DESIRABLE QUALITIES IN CHILDREN

To the extent that we desire for our children what we desire for ourselves, the data presented in this section provide a unique commentary on how the churched and unchurched differ on their evaluation of a wide range of character traits. Presented with a list of 13 qualities, persons were asked to select those three which they felt to be most desirable in a child. The most frequently selected quality, regardless of specific churched-unchurched type, was honesty. Honesty was selected by 71 percent of churched Protestants, 67 percent of unchurched Protestants, 65 percent of churched Catholics, 63 percent of unchurched Catholics, and 61 percent of those expressing no religious preference. After honesty, however, the relative ranking of specific qualities varies considerably by churched-unchurched types. For churched Protestants, the next three highest ranked qualities after honesty included (in decreasing order): obeys parents; good sense and sound judgment; and responsible. For both unchurched Protestants and churched Catholics the three most highly ranked qualities after honesty included: good sense and sound judgment; responsible; and considerate of others. For unchurched Catholics, the same three qualities were most highly ranked after honesty, but in a slightly different order. For those expressing no religious preference, the three most highly ranked qualities after honesty included: good sense and sound judgment; considerate of others; and interested in how and why things happen.

TABLE 16

OPINIONS OF THE CHURCHED AND UNCHURCHED ABOUT DESIRABLE QUALITIES
IN CHILDREN

	PROTESTANTS		CATHOLICS		NO RELIGIOUS PREFERENCE
	Churched	Unchurched	Churched	Unchurched	
PERCENT LISTING QUALITY AS ONE OF THREE MOST DESIRABLE:					
Good Manners	24	27	25	24	13
Tries Hard to Succeed	13	13	12	15	12
Honesty	71	67	65	63	61
Neatness and Cleanliness	8	10	7	6	7
Good Sense and Sound Judgment	35	38	36	39	45
Self-Control	19	17	19	12	15
Acts Like a Boy if a Boy; a Girl if a Girl	5	4	4	4	4
Gets Along Well with Other Children	15	13	16	18	13
Obeys Parents	36	27	29	26	14
Responsible	30	31	34	40	34
Considerate of Others	25	28	29	31	43
Interested in How and Why Things Happen	14	17	18	18	34
Good Student	4	6	6	5	3
(N)	(1980)	(860)	(811)	(324)	(322)

CIVIL LIBERTIES

Civil liberties, as the term is used here, specifically refers to the rights of
individuals to expound their point of view within our society freely and openly, regardless of what that point of view might be. As "test cases" of attitudes toward civil
liberties, we report data from four sets of similar questions, one set dealing with
atheism, a second dealing with socialism, a third dealing with communism, and a
fourth dealing with homosexuality. The data indicate distinct and consistent differences
among our five churched and unchurched categories. Regardless of the specific
question or specific point of view being dealt with, churched Protestants are always
least likely to be affirmative of the right to expound alternative points of view.
Unchurched Protestants and churched Catholics are somewhat more affirming of this
basic right than are churched Protestants; unchurched Catholics are even more
affirming; and those expressing no religious preference, again regardless of question
or point of view being dealt with, are most affirmative. The size of the differences

among churched and unchurched categories involved here are comparable to those found for sexual attitudes and belief in life after death, i.e., they are as large as any found in the profile.

TABLE 17

ATTITUDES OF THE CHURCHED AND UNCHURCHED ABOUT CIVIL LIBERTIES

	PROTESTANTS		CATHOLICS		NO RELIGIOUS PREFERENCE
	Churched	Unchurched	Churched	Unchurched	
A PERSON WHO IS AGAINST ALL CHURCHES AND RELIGION SHOULD:					
Be Allowed to Make a Speech in Your Community Against Churches and Religion					
Yes	55	66	69	75	85
(N)	(2673)	(1183)	(1197)	(367)	(394)
Be Allowed to Teach in a College or University					
Yes	31	43	42	57	73
(N)	(2670)	(1184)	(1195)	(367)	(392)
A Book He Wrote Against Churches and Religion Should be Removed From Your Public Library					
No	51	64	63	73	83
(N)	(2670)	(1181)	(1193)	(367)	(392)

	PROTESTANTS		CATHOLICS		NO RELIGIOUS PREFERENCE
	Churched	Unchurched	Churched	Unchurched	

A PERSON WHO FAVORS GOVERN-MENT OWNERSHIP OF ALL THE RAILROADS AND ALL BIG BUSINESS SHOULD:

Be Allowed to Make a Speech in Your Community Favoring Government Ownership of All the Railroads and Big Industries

Yes	70	79	82	84	88
(N)	(2028)	(881)	(919)	(255)	(280)

Be Allowed to Teach in a College or University

Yes	48	57	61	74	80
(N)	(2024)	(880)	(915)	(254)	(280)

A Book He Wrote Favoring Government Ownership Should be Removed from Your Public Library

No	62	74	74	77	81
(N)	(2019)	(878)	(916)	(255)	(278)

A PERSON WHO ADMITS HE IS A COMMUNIST SHOULD

Be Allowed to Make a Speech in Your Community

Yes	48	57	57	63	82
(N)	(2672)	(1183)	(1192)	(366)	(393)

	PROTESTANTS		CATHOLICS		NO RELIGIOUS PREFERENCE
	Churched	Unchurched	Churched	Unchurched	

A PERSON WHO ADMITS HE IS A COMMUNIST SHOULD (cont.)

Be Allowed to Teach in a College or University

Yes	31	40	38	50	65
(N)	(2665)	(1182)	(1192)	(365)	(393)

A Book He Wrote Should be Removed from Your Public Library

No	48	59	58	64	79
(N)	(2665)	(1182)	(1192)	(366)	(393)

A MAN WHO ADMITS HE IS A HOMOSEXUAL SHOULD:

Be Allowed to Make a Speech in Your Community

Yes	53	64	65	74	83
(N)	(1936)	(891)	(855)	(298)	(310)

Be Allowed to Teach in a College or University

Yes	41	50	52	63	76
(N)	(1936)	(892)	(854)	(298)	(310)

A Book He Wrote in Favor of Homosexuality Should be Removed from Your Public Library

No	46	56	57	66	79
(N)	(1936)	(892)	(853)	(298)	(310)

Appendix

APPENDIX A

SAMPLING TOLERANCES

In interpreting survey results, such as the percentages contained in the tables of this book, it should be remembered that all sample surveys are subject to sampling error, that is, the extent to which the results may differ from what would be obtained if the whole population had been interviewed. The size of such sampling errors depends largely on the number of interviews.

The following tables may be used in estimating sampling error appropriate to the tables found in this book. The recommended allowances have taken into account the effect of the sample design upon sampling error as estimated by the National Opinion Research Center. The recommended allowances may be interpreted as indicating the range (plus or minus the figure shown) within which the results of repeated samplings in the same time period could be expected to vary 95 percent of the time, assuming the same sampling procedure, the same interviewers, and the same questionnaire.

Table A shows how much allowance should be made for the sampling error of a single percentage. The table would be used in the following manner. Say a reported percentage is 42 for a group which includes 2500 respondents. Go to the row "Percentages near 40" in the table and then to the column headed "2500." The figure in the table at this point is two, which means that the 42 percent obtained in the sample survey is subject to a sampling error of plus or minus two points. Another way of saying it is that 95 times out of 100 the average of repeated samplings would be somewhere between 40 and 44, with the most likely figure the obtained 42.

TABLE A

RECOMMENDED ALLOWANCE FOR SAMPLING ERROR OF A PERCENTAGE

In Percentage Points
(At 95 in 100 Confidence Level)*

	GROUP SIZE										
	3500	3000	2500	2000	1500	1000	800	500	400	300	200
Percentages near 10	1	1	1	2	2	2	3	3	4	4	5
Percentages near 20	2	2	2	2	2	3	3	4	5	6	7
Percentages near 30	2	2	2	2	3	4	4	5	6	6	8
Percentages near 40	2	2	2	3	3	4	4	5	6	7	9
Percentages near 50	2	2	2	3	3	4	4	5	6	7	9
Percentages near 60	2	2	2	3	3	4	4	5	6	7	9
Percentages near 70	2	2	2	2	3	4	4	5	6	7	8
Percentages near 80	2	2	2	2	2	3	3	4	5	6	7
Percentages near 90	1	1	1	2	2	2	3	3	4	4	5

*The chances are 95 in 100 that the sampling error is not larger than the figures shown.

In comparing survey results in two groups, such as churched and unchurched Protestants, the question arises as to how large must a difference between them be before one can be reasonably sure that it reflects a real difference. Table B shows the size of the difference that should be allowed when comparing any two of our five churched and unchurched groups. For percentages near 20 or percentages near 80 use the upper half of the table. For percentages near 50 use the lower half of the table. For percentages in between, the size of the difference to be allowed for is between that shown in the two halves of the table.

Table B would be used in the following manner. Say 50 percent of churched Protestants and 40 percent of unchurched Protestants respond the same way to a question, a difference of 10 percentage points. Say also that this question was asked on all the surveys in our series so that we have a total of approximately 3500 churched Protestants and 1500 unchurched Protestants. Can it be said with any assurance that the 10 percentage point difference reflects a real difference between churched and unchurched Protestants on the question? Because the percentages are near 50, consult the lower half of the table. Because the respective sizes of the two groups are 3500 and 1500, look for the place in the lower half of the table where the row labeled "3500" and the column labeled "1500" converge. The number 4 appears there. This means that the size of difference allowance for error should be four points, and the conclusion that the percentage among churched Protestants is somewhere between six and 14 points higher than the percentage among unchurched Protestants would be wrong only about five times out of 100. In other words, there is considerable likelihood that a difference between the two groups exists in the direction observed and that it amounts to at least six percentage points, with the best estimate of the difference being the obtained 10 point difference.

If the difference between the reported percentages for two groups is not as large as the appropriate "size of the difference allowance" provided in Table B, then one cannot assume with any great confidence that the difference reflects a real difference between the two groups.

TABLE B

RECOMMENDED ALLOWANCE FOR SAMPLING ERROR OF THE DIFFERENCE BETWEEN TWO PERCENTAGES

In Percentage Points
(At 95 in 100 Confidence Level)

PERCENTAGES NEAR 20 OR PERCENTAGES NEAR 80

Size of Group	3500	3000	2500	2000	1500	1000	800	500	400	300	200
3500	2	2	3	3	3	3	4	5	5	6	7
3000		2	3	3	3	3	4	5	5	6	7
2500			3	3	3	4	4	5	5	6	7
2000				3	3	4	4	5	5	6	7
1500					4	4	4	5	5	6	7
1000						4	5	5	6	6	7
800							5	5	6	6	8
500								6	6	7	8
400									7	7	8
300										8	9
200											10

PERCENTAGES NEAR 50

Size of Group	3500	3000	2500	2000	1500	1000	800	500	400	300	200
3500	3	3	3	3	4	4	5	6	6	7	9
3000		3	3	3	4	4	5	6	6	7	9
2500			3	4	4	4	5	6	6	7	9
2000				4	4	5	5	6	7	7	9
1500					4	5	5	6	7	8	9
1000						5	6	7	7	8	9
800							6	7	7	8	9
500								8	8	9	10
400									8	9	10
300										10	11
200											12

APPENDIX B

SELECTED STUDIES IN THE DYNAMICS OF AMERICAN

CHURCH MEMBERSHIP AND PARTICIPATION

Ahlstrom, Sydney E.
  1975 A Religious History of the American People. Garden City, New York:
        Doubleday & Company, Inc.

Argyle, Michael, and Benjamin Beit-Hallahmi
  1975 The Social Psychology of Religion. London: Routledge & Kegan Paul.

Bibby, Reginald W., and Merlin B. Brinkerhoff
  1974 "Sources of Religious Involvement: Issues for Future Empirical
        Investigation," Review of Religious Research 15 (Winter): 71-79.

Campbell, Thomas C., and Yoshio Fukuyama
  1970 The Fragmented Layman: An Empirical Study of Lay Attitudes.
        Philadelphia: Pilgrim Press.

Carroll, Jackson W.; Douglas W. Johnson; and Martin Marty
  1978 Religion in America: 1950-Present. New York: Harper and Row.
  F

Carroll, Jackson W., and David A. Roozen
  1975 "Religious Participation in American Society: An Analysis of Social and
        Religious Trends and Their Interaction." Multilith. Hartford: Hartford
        Seminary Foundation.

Davis, James H., Jr.
  1962   The Outsider and the Urban Church. Philadelphia: Board of Missions of the
         Methodist Church.

Davis, James H., Jr.
  1964   "Social Bases of Participation and Non-Participation in the Contemporary
         Urban Protestant Congregation." Unpublished Ph.D. Dissertation,
         Northwestern University.

Demerath, N.J., III
  1965   Social Class in American Protestanism. Chicago: Rand McNally.

Demerath, N.J., III
  1968   "Trends and Anti-Trends in Religious Change." pp. 349-448 in Sheldon and
         Moore (eds.), Indicators of Social Change. New York: The Russell Sage
         Foundation.

Fichter, J.H.
  1954   Social Relations in the Urban Parish. Chicago: University of Chicago Press.

Gallup Opinion Index
  1967   Special Report on Religion.

  1969   Special Report on Religion (February).

  1971   Religion in America. Report No. 70 (April).

  1975   Religion in America. Report No. 114.

  1976   Religion in America. Report No. 130.

Glock, Charles Y.; Benjamin B. Ringer; and Earl R. Babbie
  1967   To Comfort and To Challenge: A Dilemma of the Contemporary Church.
         Los Angeles: University of California Press.

Greeley, Andrew M.; William C. McCready; and Kathlees McCourt
  1976   Catholic Schools in a Declining Church. Kansas City: Sheed and Ward.

Hale, J. Russell
  1977   Who Are the Unchurched? An Exploratory Study. Washington, D.C.:
         Glenmary Research Center.

Hartman, Warren J.
  1976   Membership Trends: A Study of Decline and Growth in the United Methodist
         Church, 1949-1975. Nashville: Discipleship Resources.

Hoge, Dean R.
  1974   Commitment on Campus: Changes in Religion and Values Over Five Decades.
         Philadelphia: Westminster Press.

Hoge, Dean R.
  1976   Division in the Protestant House. Philadelphia: Westminster Press.

Hoge, Dean R., and David A. Roozen
  1977   "Research on Factors Influencing Church Commitments." Unpublished.
         The Hartford Seminary Foundation.

Johnson, Douglas; Paul R. Picard; and Bernard Quinn
  1974   Churches and Church Membership in the United States: 1971. Washington,
         D.C.: Glenmary Research Center.

Kelley, Dean M.
  1972   Why Conservative Churches are Growing: A Study in Sociology of Religion.
         New York: Harper & Row.

Lenski, Gerhard
  1963   The Religious Factor: A Sociological Study of Religion's Impact on Politics,
         Economics, and Family Life. Revised Edition. Garden City, New York:
         Anchor Books.

Marty, Martin; Stuart E. Rosenburg; and Andrew M. Greeley
  1968   What Do We Believe? New York: Meredith Press.

McCready, William C.
  1972   "Faith of Our Fathers: A Study of the Process of Religious Socialization."
         Unpublished Ph.D. dissertation, University of Illinois at Chicago Circle.

Moberg, David O.
  1962   The Church as a Social Institution. Englewood Cliffs, N.J.: Prentice-Hall,
         Inc.

Moberg, David O.
  1971   "Religious Practices," pp. 551-598 in Merton P. Strommen (ed.), Research
         on Religious Development: A Comprehensive Handbook. New York:
         Hawthorn Books, Inc.

Roof, W. Clark
  1972   "The Local-Cosmopolitan Orientation and Traditional Religious Commitment,"
         Sociological Analysis 33: 1-15.

Savage, John S.
  1976   The Apathetic and Bored Church Member. Pittsford, New York: Lead
         Consultants.

Schroeder, Widick
   1975   "Age Cohorts, the Family Life Cycle, and Participation in the Voluntary
          Church in America: Implications for Membership Patterns, 1950-2000,"
          The Chicago Theological Seminary Register 65 (Fall): 13-28.

Stark, Rodney, and Charles Y. Glock
   1970   American Piety: The Nature of Religious Commitment. Los Angeles:
          University Press.

Committee on Membership Trends, United Presbyterian Church
   1976   Membership Trends. New York: General Assembly Mission Council,
          United Presbyterian Church in the U.S.A.

Wagner, C. Peter
   1976   Your Church Can Grow. Glendale, California: Regal.

Wuthnow, Robert
   1976a The Consciousness Reformation. Berkeley: University of California Press.

   1976b "Recent Patterns of Secularization: A Problem of Generations?" American
          Sociological Review 41 (October): 850-67.

A Companion Study...

WHO ARE THE UNCHURCHED?
AN EXPLORATORY STUDY

by J. Russell Hale, Lutheran Theological
Seminary at Gettysburg

Describes what the unchurched have to say
about themselves, based on 156 in-depth
interviews in six widely-separated counties.
Contains background on the six counties, a
provisional classification of the unchurched,
and liberal quotations from the interviews
themselves. [105 pages]

Published by the Glenmary Research Center,
4606 East-West Highway, Washington, DC
20014. Price: $2.00, including postage.